NORTH CAROLINA GEOGRAPHY

NORTH CAROLINA HAS THREE GEOGRAPHIC REGIONS: THE BLUE RIDGE MOUNTAINS IN THE WEST, THE PIEDMONT'S ROLLING HILLS OF FARMLAND IN THE MIDDLE, AND LOW COASTAL PLAINS BY THE OCEAN IN THE EAST. NORTH CAROLINA IS 560 MILES WIDE, SO WEATHER CAN CHANGE A LOT FROM ONE END TO THE OTHER! THE AVERAGE AUGUST TEMPERATURE IN THE MOUNTAINS IS 65 DEGREES BUT IN THE COASTAL PLAIN IS IN THE 90S.

N.C.'S **MOUNT MITCHELL** IS THE HIGHEST PEAK EAST OF THE MISSISSIPPI RIVER.

THE BLUE RIDGE IS PART OF THE **APPALACHIAN MOUNTAINS**.

"PIEDMONT" IS A FRENCH WORD MEANING "FOOT OF THE MOUNTAIN."

THE COASTAL PLAIN HAS A STRING OF BARRIER ISLANDS GOOD FOR VACATIONING.

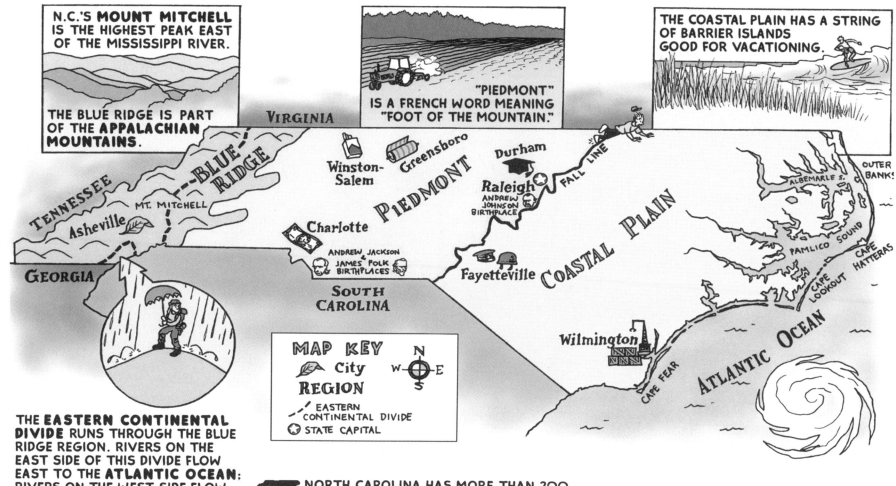

THE **EASTERN CONTINENTAL DIVIDE** RUNS THROUGH THE BLUE RIDGE REGION. RIVERS ON THE EAST SIDE OF THIS DIVIDE FLOW EAST TO THE **ATLANTIC OCEAN**; RIVERS ON THE WEST SIDE FLOW WEST TO THE **GULF OF MEXICO**.

MAP KEY

City

REGION

- - - EASTERN CONTINENTAL DIVIDE

⭐ STATE CAPITAL

NORTH CAROLINA HAS MORE THAN 200 WATERFALLS. **WHITEWATER FALLS** IN TRANSYLVANIA COUNTY IS THE HIGHEST WATERFALL ON AMERICA'S EAST COAST.

THE BILTMORE ESTATE IN **ASHEVILLE** IS THE LARGEST PRIVATE HOUSE IN THE WORLD – IT HAS 250 ROOMS!

THE **CAPE HATTERAS LIGHTHOUSE** IS THE TALLEST LIGHTHOUSE IN THE UNITED STATES.

GRANDFATHER MOUNTAIN HAS THE NATION'S HIGHEST SWINGING BRIDGE, ONE MILE UP IN THE AIR!

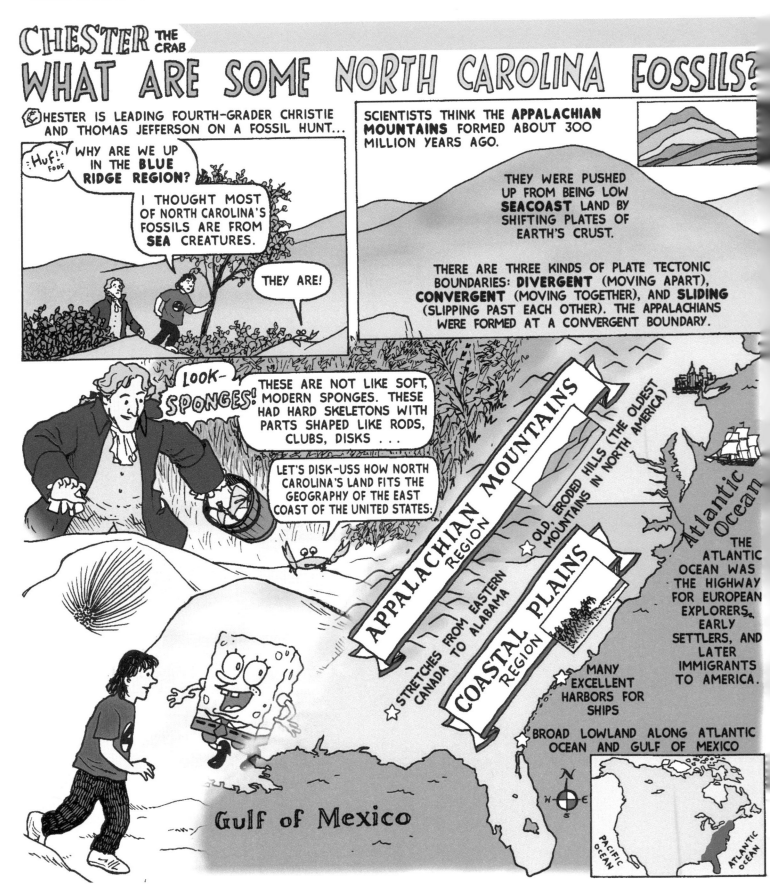

CHAPTER 1

COLONIAL CAROLINA

The **first known European exploration of North Carolina** happens during the summer of **1524**. A Florentine navigator named **Giovanni da Verrazano is working for France** and explores the coastal area. Between 1540 and 1570 some **Spanish explorers** come up from their Florida territory to check things out. But it is **the English** who try to settle the coast of Carolina . . .

North Carolina's tribes are in three language groups: Iroquoian, Siouan, and Algonquian. (Obj. 2.01)

The first colony in Carolina, led by Ralph Lane, ends in failure. (Obj. 3.02)

The 110 settlers in 1587 include 17 women and 9 children. (Obj. 3.03)

No one has ever successfully explained what happened to "The Lost Colony." (Obj. 3.03)

WHERE DID "THE LOST COLONY" GO?

GOVERNOR JOHN WHITE CANNOT GET A SHIP TO RETURN TO **ROANOKE COLONY** IN **1588** AS HE HAD PLANNED.

WHY NOT??

The SPANISH ARMADA Attacks!

ENGLAND'S QUEEN **ELIZABETH I** ORDERS EVERY AVAILABLE SHIP TO FIGHT OFF THE INVADERS. ENGLAND WINS THIS BATTLE!

AFTER THE WAR, FEW ENGLISHMEN CARE ABOUT AMERICAN COLONIES. WHITE MUST RAISE MONEY FOR SUPPLIES AND SHIPS HIMSELF. HE DOESN'T GET BACK TO ROANOKE UNTIL **1590**.

NO ONE IS HERE, AND THE COLONY'S SMALL BOATS ARE MISSING.

BOYD '02

CROATOAN

LOOK! THE WORD "CROATOAN." WHAT DOES IT MEAN??

IT COULD MEAN THREE THINGS...

1. THE COLONISTS STARTED FOR CROATOAN ISLAND BUT WERE KILLED BY INDIANS FIRST.

2. THE COLONISTS WENT TO LIVE ON CROATOAN ISLAND SOUTH OF HERE BUT WERE KILLED BY SPANISH RAIDERS.

BOOM

3. THE COLONISTS WENT TO THE MAINLAND TO LIVE WITH THE CROATOAN INDIANS.

THESE AREN'T LIKELY. CROATOAN ISLAND IS BAD FOR GROWING CROPS AND IS EXPOSED TO OCEAN STORMS.

TWENTY YEARS AFTER ROANOKE, ENGLAND STARTS A COLONY THAT SURVIVES: **JAMESTOWN**. SETTLERS THERE HEAR RUMORS FROM INDIANS THAT THE ROANOKE SETTLERS ARE STILL ALIVE, SOMEWHERE...

JAMESTOWN

HEY! WAIT!!

NO ONE KNOWS WHAT REALLY HAPPENED TO THE "LOST COLONY" OF ROANOKE. IT PROVES HISTORY IS NOT A STRAIGHT MARCH OF PROGRESS. THERE ARE MANY TWISTS AND TURNS!

CHESTER THE CRAB

WHAT WORK DID COLONISTS DO?

SHIPBUILDING
IRONWORKS
TOBACCO
RICE
WHEAT

EUROPEANS WHO SETTLE THE EAST COAST OF NORTH AMERICA PICK JOBS THAT FIT THEIR REGIONS. THEY USE THE NATURAL RESOURCES THEY FIND AROUND THEM.

13-PIECE PUZZLE

NEW ENGLAND

THE BUSINESS ON THIS JAGGED, COLD COASTLINE IS BASED ON SAILING SHIPS. PORT CITIES SUCH AS BOSTON SUPPLY AND BUILD SHIPS. MANY SAILORS USE THESE SHIPS TO FISH THE ATLANTIC OCEAN. OTHER NEW ENGLANDERS USE SHIPS TO TRADE THINGS ACROSS THE OCEAN - INCLUDING SLAVES FROM AFRICA FOR THE SOUTHERN PLANTATIONS.

Mid-Atlantic

FARMERS HERE RAISE ANIMALS AND GROW GRAIN. PEOPLE IN THE GROWING CITIES BUILD FURNITURE, RUN PRINTING PRESSES, AND MAKE TOOLS. FISHERMEN ALSO DO WELL ALONG THIS COASTLINE.

The South

THIS ECONOMY HAS LARGE FARMS CALLED PLANTATIONS. THESE GROW CROPS SOLD FOR CASH (TOBACCO AND COTTON). RICH WHITE PEOPLE LIVING IN PLANTATION MANSIONS USE SLAVES TO WORK IN THESE HOT, HUMID FIELDS.

SO THERE ARE SOME REAL DIFFERENCES IN THE COLONIES NOW: BIG FARMERS VERSUS SMALL FARMERS, CITY PEOPLE VERSUS COUNTRY PEOPLE, BLACKS VERSUS WHITES.

HOW DOES IT ALL COME TOGETHER?

NEXT:
WHY I HATE BRITAIN

BOYD '00

9

CHESTER THE CRAB

WHY DID COLONISTS FIGHT BRITAIN?

⚓ SHIPBUILDING
🔺 IRONWORKS
🌿 TOBACCO
🌾 RICE
🌾 WHEAT

IN THE 1760s THE COLONIAL POPULATION IS ABOUT 2 MILLION. THE 13 COLONIES HAVE LEGISLATURES OF LOCAL POLITICIANS MAKING LOCAL LAWS. THEY ALSO HAVE GOVERNORS APPOINTED BY THE KING TO WATCH THESE COLONIAL POLITICIANS CLOSELY.

13-PIECE PUZZLE

NEW ENGLAND

THIS REGION HAS MANY SMALL VILLAGES. CITIZENS GET TOGETHER IN TOWN MEETINGS TO DECIDE LAWS OR POLITICAL QUESTIONS. THESE PEOPLE GET MAD WHEN BRITAIN FORCES THEM TO KEEP BRITISH SOLDIERS IN THEIR HOMES ("QUARTERING").

SLEEPOVER!!

Mid-Atlantic

THE MARKET TOWNS HERE FOCUS ON TRADE. MOST COLONISTS IN BUSINESS HATE BRITAIN'S **NAVIGATION ACTS.** THE ACTS ARE LAWS THAT REQUIRE ALL COLONIAL TRADE TO GO THROUGH BRITAIN FIRST. THIS SLOWS SHIPS DOWN AND MAKES THINGS MORE EXPENSIVE TO SELL AND BUY.

COSTS

The South

BECAUSE BIG PLANTATIONS TAKE UP SO MUCH LAND HERE, THERE ARE FEW CITIES. THE POLITICAL LIFE HERE IS BASED ON COUNTY COURTHOUSES.

NO ONE WANTS TO PAY BRITAIN'S **STAMP ACT** TAX ON COURTHOUSE PAPERS OR TOBACCO BARRELS. VIRGINIA'S PATRICK HENRY CONVINCES HIS COLONY AND MANY OTHERS TO FIGHT THE STAMP ACT OF 1765.

NO TAXATION WITHOUT REPRESENTATION!!

SO BY 1776, THE 13 COLONIES ALL HAVE REASONS TO WORK TOGETHER AGAINST BRITAIN.

THANKS FOR HELPING ME PUT THE PIECES TOGETHER, CHESTER!

BOYD '00

CAROLINA IN THE 1800's

After the Revolutionary War brings freedom to North Carolina, the **first state capitol** is built in Raleigh in 1794 and North Carolina gives up its western lands in 1790 (they will become the state of Tennessee). Before the Civil War, two North Carolina natives become **president of the United States: Andrew Jackson (1829-1837) and James K. Polk (1845-1849)**. Then North Carolina secedes and joins the **Confederacy** in May 1861; it gains its nickname "**The Tar Heel State**" during **Civil War** battles in which its soldiers stick on the battlefield longer than troops from other Southern states . . .

President James Polk secures Oregon and Texas lands during his time in the White House. (Obj. 4.05)

CHESTER THE CRAB

WHEN DID OREGON BECOME A STATE?

CHESTER AND 1,000 MEN, WOMEN, AND KIDS REACH THE OREGON TERRITORY AFTER 177 DAYS ON THE TRAIL!

YIPPEE! WE MADE IT TO OUR NEW LAND! OUR TROUBLES ARE OVER!!

NO WAY, JOSE! IT IS NOVEMBER. IF YOU WANT A HOME WITH A ROOF, HELP CUT DOWN SOME OF THESE GIANT TREES!

BOYD '03

SOON, THOUSANDS OF AMERICANS TAKE THE OREGON TRAIL WEST. . .

FORT VANCOUVER

REMEMBER: **BRITAIN** AND THE UNITED STATES HAVE SHARED THIS LAND SINCE 1818.

WELL, THERE ARE A LOT **MORE** AMERICANS HERE NOW. WE WANT TO BE A STATE!

RUSSIA'S **ALASKA** TERRITORY GOES DOWN TO THE LATITUDE 54°40'. BRITISH FUR TRAPPERS WANT TO DRAW THEIR BOUNDARY WITH THE U.S. AT THE COLUMBIA RIVER. AMERICANS START TO DEMAND:

54°40' OR FIGHT!

54° 40'

49° 0'

Pacific Ocean

British Canada

Oregon Country

United States

COLUMBIA RIVER

WILL THERE BE A WAR? AMERICANS ELECT **JAMES POLK** PRESIDENT IN 1844. HE CALLS FOR MORE LAND.

GOD HAS GIVEN AMERICA A "**MANIFEST DESTINY**" TO SPREAD FROM ATLANTIC OCEAN TO PACIFIC OCEAN. IT IS OUR DESTINY TO TAKE LAND FROM INDIANS, MEXICANS, BRITISH

WAR IS AVOIDED WHEN POLK ACCEPTS AN OREGON BOUNDARY AT THE LATITUDE 49° IN 1846.

YeeHA!

OREGON IS THE 33RD STATE, ADMITTED IN 1859. END

5

North Carolinian Andrew Johnson tries to put America back together after the Civil War. (Obj. 4.05)

HOW FREE WERE THE FREED MEN?

ANDREW JOHNSON

IS **PRESIDENT** OF THE UNITED STATES AFTER THE **CIVIL WAR**.

Radical Republican

CONGRESSMEN ARE LED BY **THADDEUS STEVENS** OF PENNSYLVANIA.

IT IS TIME TO BRING OUR FAMILY TOGETHER AGAIN. THESE SOUTHERN REPRESENTATIVES ARE READY TO REJOIN CONGRESS.

ONE OF THOSE MEN WAS VICE-PRESIDENT OF THE CONFEDERACY!! WE DIDN'T FIGHT A GRISLY WAR SO THOSE TRAITORS COULD TAKE OVER CONGRESS!! WE WILL **NOT** LET THEM IN!

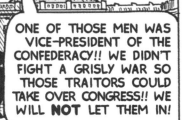

IN **1866** ELECTIONS, NORTHERN "RADICAL" REPUBLICANS GAIN POWER IN THE **UNITED STATES CONGRESS**.

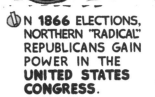

NOW WE HAVE ENOUGH VOTES TO OVERRIDE THE PRESIDENT'S VETO. WE CAN DO WHATEVER WE WANT!

OUR PLAN FOR **RECONSTRUCTING** THE SOUTH IS: STATES MUST RATIFY THESE AMENDMENTS BEFORE WE LET THEM BACK INTO THE UNION.

Fourteenth Amendment

THIS ERASES THE SUPREME COURT'S "DRED SCOTT" DECISION (WHICH SAID SLAVES DO NOT HAVE RIGHTS). THIS AMENDMENT GRANTS **CITIZENSHIP** TO ALL PERSONS BORN IN THE U.S., REGARDLESS OF **RACE**.

Fifteenth Amendment

THIS GIVES ALL AMERICAN MEN THE RIGHT TO **VOTE**, REGARDLESS OF RACE OR COLOR OR "PREVIOUS CONDITION OF SERVITUDE" (THAT MEANS SLAVERY).

In Reality... FREED SLAVES DO NOT GET EQUAL PROTECTION UNDER THE LAWS. BLACKS STILL CANNOT TESTIFY IN MANY TRIALS.

In Reality... WHITES KEEP EX-SLAVES FROM VOTING BY USING **READING TESTS** OR **POLL TAXES**. FEW POOR BLACKS CAN AFFORD TO PAY A TAX TO VOTE.

CHESTER THE CRAB

| 1860 LINCOLN ELECTED | 1863 GETTYSBURG | 1869 TRANSCONTINENTAL RR | 1886 |

WHERE DID RAILROADS CARRY TEXTILES?

ANOTHER NORTH CAROLINA INDUSTRY THAT GROWS OUT OF NEW RAILROAD CONNECTIONS IS THE TEXTILE BUSINESS.

TEXTILES ARE CLOTHES, SHEETS, TABLECLOTHS — ANYTHING MADE WITH FIBERS.

FARMERS IN THE DEEP SOUTH CONTINUE TO GROW COTTON AFTER THE WAR. NEW RAILROADS CARRY COTTON AND SHEEP'S WOOL UP TO NORTH CAROLINA'S **PIEDMONT REGION**.

TEXTILE FACTORIES POP UP ON NORTH CAROLINA'S MANY RIVERS BECAUSE THEY CAN USE THE RIVERS FOR POWER.

MILLS HIRE WORKERS FROM PIEDMONT FARM FAMILIES THAT ARE TIRED OF THEIR ENDLESS CYCLE OF CROP DEBT.

CHAPTER 3

KNOW YOUR WRIGHTS

As the 1800s come to a close, dozens of people around the world are trying to solve the problem of giving mankind the power to fly through the air in a **heavier-than-air craft**. Two bicycle makers from Ohio decide the best place to try their own aircraft ideas is on the windy, sandy dunes of **Kitty Hawk, North Carolina . . .**

Like many others, the Wright brothers test their flight ideas by using gliders first. (Obj. 4.05)

The Wright brothers also like Kitty Hawk, NC, because it is quiet and private. (Obj. 4.05)

The Wright brothers' flight in N.C. changes the way people think about transportation. (Obj. 4.05)

HOW LONG WAS THE 1ST WRIGHT FLIGHT?

WILBUR AND ORVILLE WRIGHT RETURN TO KILL DEVIL HILLS, NORTH CAROLINA, IN **1903**. THEY HAVE A GLIDER WITH A MOTOR THEY BUILT THEMSELVES IN THEIR BICYCLE SHOP IN DAYTON, OHIO.

HAVE YOU HEARD? SAMUEL PIERPONT LANGLEY'S AERODROME JUST **CRASHED** INTO THE POTOMAC RIVER. HE FAILED TO FLY!

OUCH! THAT CRAFT COST $73,000.

WE'VE SPENT ONLY $1,000 ON OURS! LET'S GET GOING BEFORE WINTER HITS.

ON DEC. 17, PUDDLES AROUND THEIR CAMP ARE FROZEN. WINDS ARE HIGH.

LET'S DO IT.

ORVILLE CLIMBS ABOARD. THE "WRIGHT FLYER" CLATTERS DOWN A 60-FOOT RAIL.

KLAKLIKLAKLACKLIKLAKLAKLAKKKKLAK

BOYD'02

HE FLIES!

HE GOES 120 FEET IN 12 SECONDS — ABOUT THE TIME IT TAKES TO SAY:

THIS IS THE FIRST FLIGHT BY A HEAVIER-THAN-AIR MACHINE CARRYING A PERSON THAT
• RAISES ITSELF BY ITS OWN POWER
• SAILS FORWARD WITHOUT SLOWING
• LANDS AT A POINT AS HIGH AS IT STARTED!

THIS FIRST FLIGHT ISN'T FAR, BUT IT POINTS THE WAY TO SPACE SHUTTLES!
END

TALE OF THE DOGWOOD

North Carolina has many symbols - pictures that stand for something else. The **official state vegetable is the sweet potato, the state bird is the cardinal, and the state tree is the pine**. The **state flower** also comes from a tree - the **dogwood**. The dogwood tree can be found across North Carolina, from the mountains to the coast. People enjoy the dogwood's white or pink bracts, which appear in springtime.

Dogwood trees are one of the natural resources of North Carolina. (Obj. 1.01)

CHESTER THE CRAB
HOW HARD IS DOGWOOD WOOD?

CHESTER IS ON A **STATE FLOWER** FIELD TRIP.

ONE OF THE THINGS THE NORTH CAROLINA DOGWOOD IS KNOWN FOR IS ITS HARD WOOD.

pinch

WHACK

SORRY!

ITS SCIENTIFIC NAME IS "CORNUS FLORIDA." IT COMES FROM LATIN'S "CORNU," MEANING "HORN" — BECAUSE ITS WOOD IS AS HARD AS ANIMAL HORNS!

THE NAME "DOGWOOD" MAY COME FROM AN OLD ENGLISH WORD, "DAGGE" — A SHARP OBJECT!

THE NAME MAY ALSO COME FROM THE BARK ON THE DOGWOOD'S TRUNK. PEOPLE BOIL THIS BARK TO MAKE A SHAMPOO THAT KILLS PESTS IN A DOG'S HAIR.

THE WOOD OF THIS TREE IS SO GOOD AT TAKING SUDDEN WHACKS THAT IT HAS LONG BEEN USED TO MAKE GOLF CLUB HEADS, MALLETS, AND CHISEL HANDLES. THESE TOOLS ARE EXAMPLES OF HOW IMPORTANT TREES ARE TO HUMANS. (WE ALSO TURN TREES INTO LUMBER TO BUILD OUR HOUSES.)

WE GET WOOD FROM THE TRUNK AND BRANCHES OF A TREE. THE TRUNK AND BRANCHES ARE ITS **STEM**.

IT'S COOL HOW THE BRANCHES TWIST AS THEY GROW OUT. WHY DO THEY DO THAT??

A DOGWOOD IN THE FOREST TWISTS TO FIND PATCHES OF SUNLIGHT. IT NEEDS TO GET ITS LEAVES IN THE LIGHT!

BOK

BOYD '02

NEXT: Photo Phinish

CHESTER THE CRAB
WHO POLLINATES DOGWOOD TREES?

SO FAR WE HAVE STUDIED THE DOGWOOD'S ROOTS, THE STEM, THE LEAVES ... BUT WHAT ABOUT A DOGWOOD'S FLOWERS?? IT'S THE **STATE FLOWER**, RIGHT?!!

IS THIS THE FLOWER? IT'S BEAUTIFUL!

YES, IT IS BEAUTIFUL.

NO, IT IS **NOT** THE FLOWER!

THESE FOUR THINGS ARE "BRACTS." THESE SPECIAL LEAVES SHIELD THE SMALL DOGWOOD FLOWER FROM WINTER COLD.

YOU SEE THESE BRACTS IN LATE MARCH OR APRIL. THEY OPEN TO LET THE PLANT'S REPRODUCTION GO TO WORK.

STAMEN THESE PRODUCE POLLEN.

STIGMA POLLEN MUST FALL HERE TO DEVELOP SEEDS IN THE OVARY.

PETAL

OVARY OVULES HERE BECOME SEEDS.

SEPAL THE HOUSING OF THE DEVELOPING FLOWER.

HITCHHIKERS

OTHER PLANTS LET THE WIND HELP THEM POLLINATE.

THE DOGWOOD'S UNFOLDING IN EARLY SPRING ATTRACTS INSECTS. THE BUGS TRAVEL FROM FLOWER TO FLOWER GATHERING FOOD. BUT AS THEY TRAVEL, THEIR FEET CARRY **POLLEN** FROM STAMENS TO STIGMA.

THIS IS CALLED **POLLINATION**. IT IS HOW A PLANT MAKES SEEDS TO MAKE MORE COPIES OF ITSELF, SINCE THERE ARE NO DATING SERVICES FOR PLANTS. THE DOGWOOD TREE HAS A FUNNY WAY OF SPREADING ITS SEEDS AROUND...

NEXT: The POOP Scoop

BOYD '02

CHESTER THE CRAB
HOW DO DOGWOOD SEEDS TRAVEL?

CHESTER IS EXPLAINING TREE SCIENCE:

AFTER THE PRETTY BRACTS FALL OFF AND THE POLLINATION IS DONE, THE REAL WORK BEGINS!

THE OVARY AT THE BASE OF THE DOGWOOD FLOWER'S PISTIL RIPENS. IT BECOMES A BRIGHT RED, EGG-SHAPED FRUIT CALLED A "DRUPE."

YUMMY FRUIT

SEED

THIS IS HOW THE DOGWOOD HAS ADAPTED TO GET ITS **SEED** SPREAD AROUND AS FAR AS POSSIBLE.

IN THE FALL THE DRUPE BECOMES JUICY FOOD FOR A SQUIRREL...

CHOMP

... OR A BIRD.

GULP

TREES AND OTHER PLANTS PROVIDE HOMES AND FOOD FOR MANY ANIMALS. WITH THE DOGWOOD TREE, WE SEE A GOOD EXAMPLE OF HOW PLANTS AND ANIMALS NEED EACH OTHER. THEY ARE **INTERDEPENDENT**.

NOW WE WAIT.

WAIT FOR WHAT? WHAT HAPPENS NOW?

YEAH, WHERE IS THE SEED FOR A NEW TREE??

POOP

EEEYEEW

THERE IS THE START OF YOUR NEXT DOGWOOD TREE! THE SEED IS ALL FERTILIZED AND READY TO GROW!! END